COSTA RICA

THE LAND BETWEEN TWO OCEANS

WHITE STAR PUBLISHERS

Text
Simona Stoppa

Contents

1 Among Costa Rica's 850 identified bird species is the hummingbird, which is indispensable for the survival of many plants and flowers in the lower reaches of the forest. Up to 70-90 percent of these plants' ability to reproduce depends solely on the collaboration they receive from certain other animals.

2-3 The Pacific coastline that extends for 631 miles (1016 km) from the frontier with Nicaragua to that of Panama, differs from the Atlantic one because of its much indented shoreline with its many gulfs, small bays, lagoons and peninsulas.

4-5 Using the hunting method typical of felines, jaguars silently creep up furtively on their prey, launching a sudden final attack from very close quarters. This animal is capable of traveling at very high speed for brief periods, but has little stamina over extended distances.

6 In Costa Rica, many decorative elements are lavished on the carretas, *the old wooden agricultural carts painted meticulously with lively colors, as well as on other wooden articles handcrafted by local artisans. There is also a flourishing activity in the decoration and creation of ceramics and textiles. The best-known craft center in Costa Rica is the small city of Sarchí, located on the highland plains to the north.*

7 In July of 1968 the Arenal volcano erupted with heavy lava flows that killed

dozens of people and destroyed many surrounding villages. Ever since then, the volcano continues to produce enormous columns of ash, powerful explosions and rivers of white-hot lava, interspersing them from time to time with simple flashes.

8-9 On the beach in Manuel Antonio National Park, on Costa Rica's Pacific coast, local artisans sell colorful pareos to visitors, who are plentiful in this area. The Park's natural beauty, as can be seen from the promontory and the variety of animal species, make it a preferred destination for tourists.

10-11 The huge Heliconia flowers provide an excellent support for the red-eyed tree frogs (Agalychnis Callidryas) that live in the dense forests along the waterways. They are extremely brightly colored amphibians: the predominant body color is a brilliant green, often dotted with blue and yellow spots, with orange feet and huge red eyes. The male differs from the female not in its coloring but in its smaller size.

12-13 The Santa Elena Cloud Forest Reserve is a fascinating forest with high humidity located along the Cordillera de Tilarán, not far from the more famous Monteverde Reserve. The dense rain forest, often 130 ft (40 m) high, grows luxuriantly at 3280 ft (1000 m), being constantly covered by clouds. Following the numerous footpaths in the reserve, the visitor meets animals of every species and, if cloud cover lifts, sees the Arenal volcano.

© 2008 White Star S.p.A.
Via C. Sassone, 22/24
13100 Vercelli, Italy
www.whitestar.it

TRANSLATION
Neale Maddalena

ISBN 978-88-544-0363-5

REPRINTS:
1 2 3 4 5 6   12 11 10 09 08

Printed in Singapore
Color separation: Areagroup media, Milan

Introduction

Sweet and bitter. Brilliant and obscure. Violent and tranquil. Yet it's always "rrrica," or "rrrich," with the rolled "r" used by those who not only refer to the Republic of Costa Rica but also embrace it and drink it all in. By those, in fact, relentlessly in search of the *pura vida*, forever spontaneous and natural, to the lively rhythms of Latin dance and the tumult of a clamorous and exuberant nature. Costa Rica, a baptismal name whose origins date back to 1502 when Christopher Columbus, while sailing in search of the fabled El Dorado, stumbled upon the country's Atlantic coast. Once on land, the Spanish settlers were blinded by the gold trinkets worn by the *Indios*, a probable sign of the presence of a rich empire. In reality, what they found were small native settlements and an unimaginable expanse of rain forest. The same, extravagant vegetation has now become the standard of the *Ticos*, drunken natives wandering along high mist-bound valleys, through savannas, mangrove swamps, mountain chains, volcanoes, coral cliffs, green islands and mysterious forests.

The country has a population of approximately 4 million people, shut into a treasure chest of little more than 31,000 sq. miles (51,000 sq. km), barely larger than Switzerland. It's a place where education and health services are free and guaranteed to everyone. A nation that has never liked either gunpowder or military ranks; a nation that has not had an army since 1949 and feels confident and safe enough to do without one. A nation that has elected to devote itself, throughout the years and under changing governments, to a single, enlightened mission: that of preserving nature by declaring a quarter of its territory protected land. Costa Rica churns out numbers and awards and has put together twenty national parks, thirteen wildlife reserves and dozens of nature areas. The census of mammals and birds, insects and amphibians, trees and plants are repeated endlessly, because here in the tropics there is no covering cement nor the filtered effects of man: in Costa Rica nature is both supreme yet daughter to itself. Untouched by anthropomorphic hands: nature is at its most pure and takes in 6 percent of the various biological species of the entire planet.

Just to cross the protected wildlife reserves and other areas set aside for biological, forest and *Indios* preservation makes it impossible to avoid intoxication: the sweet perfumes are carried away through the air by animals invisible to the eye but still audible in near and distant echoes.

Trees under siege from bromeliads, giant ferns, brilliant orchids and creepers of all types reach out toward the sky for over 130 ft (40 m). There are at least 900 different species of trees, 1300 varieties of orchids, some being endemic and one adopted as the national flower, the "Guaria Morada" *(Cattleya skinneri)*; this is a giant orchid, sublime in form, fragrance and color. There is also a national tree, the Guanacaste, also known as the "ear tree" due to the curling of its leaves, and a national bird, the "Yigüirro," a grey-colored thrush that mates in the rainy season and so symbolizes the earth's fertility.

But the counting doesn't end here. Here is another cascade of numbers. The more than 200 species of mammals that populate Costa Rica include jaguars, pumas, monkeys, sloths, anteaters and raccoons; there are 800 species of birds, including 50 hummingbirds and 15 parrots, and reptiles, amphibians and insects make up a further 40,000 different species, of which 3000 are butterflies.

This vast garden between the oceans, this bridge of land in the middle of the American continent, is bordered by Nicaragua to the north and Panama to the southeast. It possesses two sea outlooks: one coastline overlooks the Pacific Ocean and the other the Caribbean Sea. A country that is at the same time male and female: its central skeleton, bony, steep and harsh, is softened by smooth and sinuous hips laid open to be molded by the sea. Majestic cordilleras and ferocious volcanoes give way to plains, dotted by rainforests, and then gradually descend towards

the sand-dusted beaches of the coast. This is a nature that gives up its own savage harshness wherever humankind appears, weighed down with needs and foolish ambitions.

The land has kept one of its jewels at a distance, out in the open sea, to preserve it from any element of risk – just as with species on the verge of extinction. This is the Isla del Coco, the biggest uninhabited island in the world and possibly the most beautiful. Located approximately 300 miles (500 km) southwest of the Pacific coast, it has been part of Costa Rica since 1869 and has always fed the collective imagination with dreams of a priceless treasure. Since first appearing on maps in the 16th century, it became the landing place for whalers and pirates, stocking up on water and the island's coconuts, and burying treasure after treasure. Of the so-called "loot of Lima" – transported to the island by Captain William Thompson in 1820, during the war of independence between Chile and Peru – down to the immense treasure stolen from a Spanish galleon by the British pirate Bennett Graham, better known as Benito Bonito, nothing has as yet been recovered, despite hundreds of search expeditions. In 1881, the illicit activities of these pirates inspired Robert Louis Stevenson to write *Treasure Island* and later, prompted by the steep faces and impenetrable forest of this remote rock, Michael Crichton wrote the best-seller *Jurassic Park*. But its fame is not

14 Not even the cliffs can resist in Costa Rica. The savage tropical nature always contrives to prevail over everything. The erosion of the rocks carves out small inlets protected from wind and ocean currents, preserving a wild and undisturbed natural environment.

14-15 The Caribbean coast is punctuated by small fishing villages hidden by the thick vegetation that extends down to the shore. Fishing and employment on the banana plantations are the only means of support for the inhabitants of these villages.

16 *White Magic is one of the waterfalls in the La Paz Nature Park, located near Vara Blanca. The park takes the name of the river which runs for almost 4600 ft (1400 m) down the sides of the volcano, dramatizing its descent with a number of spectacular waterfalls.*

17 top *The four hot springs that supply the thermal resort of Tabacón, at the foot of the Arenal volcano, provide an ideal setting for relaxing and enjoying the natural firework displays offered by the volcano. There* are ten individual baths where the visitor can stay pleasantly immersed at temperatures ranging from 90° to 104° Fahrenheit (23° to 40° Celsius).

17 bottom *The jaguar (Panthera onca) is a feline that easily disguises itself against the background of the rain forests of Costa Rica. Notwithstanding its overall dimensions – it can weigh over 200 lbs (100 kg) and exceed 6 ft (2 m) in length – it is easier to find its footprints or listen to its roar than to actually see it.*

18 and 18-19 *The interior of the Teatro Nacional of San José, with its precious marble and rich decorations, is as impressive as its external façade, Renaissance in style and surmounted by three statues. Construction began in* 1891 *and it opened to the public on October 21, 1897, with* Faust. *The Teatro Nacional is considered the most beautiful building in the country, famous also for its symphony orchestra and its theater and dance company.*

merely confined to legends and motion pictures: declared a National Park in its entirety, the Isla del Coco is a tropical garden bursting with more than 70 species of endemic animals and plants, and pierced by over 100 waterfalls cascading into the extremely thick jungle to form small, crystal-clear lakes. Above all, this tiny slice of land lies in the midst of immense depths, a much sought-after home for hundreds of hammerhead sharks, turtles, manta rays, spotted devil fish and whale sharks. An exaggeration of life, pulsating in no more than 15 sq. miles (24 sq. km) and held at bay by three volcanic cones. Silent, unlike the mountain ranges that run down the mainland dividing the country by means of a natural weather barrier: while the Caribbean area is overwhelmed all year long under a hot and humid climate with frequent rains, the Pacific coast region stays enjoyably dry from December to April, collecting its rain during the rest of the year.

From the Cordillera de Guanacaste in the north, defined by a spectacular series of volcanoes reaching heights of 6500 ft (2000 m), the visitor gets pitched across to the Cordillera de Tilaran overlooking the Arenal Lagoon, so perfect as to appear unreal. This is an artificial lake dominated by a volcano that could not have wished for a better cone. Rising 5356 ft (1633 m) in height, no artist could have shaped it better. Just as no devil could have embodied it with fiercer fury and ardor. The asphalt strip of the Panamerican Highway, pitted and holed, lead the way to hell: sudden and violent explosions, white-hot clouds, liquid fire setting out to conquer the earth. Nature's attack on nature itself. These repositories of fascination have trembled, smoked and burned since 1968. These eruptions are difficult to predict, even though monitored day by day. The Arenal is not only the most active volcano of the country but among the most active in the world. When at its foot, submerged in the hot springs of Tabacón and surrounded by the darkest night, nothing in the world can be found to compare with one of the most beautiful light and sound shows on the entire planet: the blackness, only broken by the luminosity of white-hot lapilli, is no longer black. Sudden explosions light up the scene all around until the Great Master elects to shut himself down in a renewed silence.

But much more is to be found here besides fire: a forest, dressed in green and veiled in white, competes to share the scene. This is the "Reserva Biológica Bosque Nuboso Monteverde," a private, age-old forest where low cloud and the muffled sounds of mysterious animals permeate the thick density of contorted trees. An oasis in expansion, protected by the Monteverde Conservation League, financed with donations from all over the world and dedicated to protecting as much land as possible.

The columns of ashes and the lava streams flow incessantly also along the Cordillera Central. The Poás, from its commanding height of 8869 ft (2704 m), glows under its rock-lined walls and amazes visitors with its enormous crater, a smoking and bubbling cauldron, 1000 ft (300 m) deep and 1 mile (1.5 km) wide. Alongside, to soften this angry setting, a misty forest of contorted trees vibrates to the resonant notes of flame-throated hummingbirds, yellow-eyed blackbirds and the extremely rare quetzal.

The Irazu volcano, rising 11,256 ft (3432 m), is the country's most active eruptive center. Though now given only to small fumaroles, in 1963 it reached the maximum of its expressiveness. Its last, terrible show the eruption covered with up to 20 inches (50 cm) of ashes the cities of San José, Cartago and most of the Valle Centrale. Here, the fire meets another natural barrier, the Meseta Central: a strip of land between the Cordillera Central and the Cordillera de Talamanca that has never known desolation, thanks to such waterways as the Chirripó, the Sarapiquí, the Grande de Tárcoles and the Rio Reventazon.

The mountainous backbone spreads southeast to create the Cordillera de Talamanca, harsher and more remote than its sisters, as well as more ancient from a geological standpoint. Many of its peaks exceed 10,000 ft (3000 m), reaching up to the 12,530 ft (3820 m) of Cerro Chirripó, offering a view that melts into the global embrace of the oceans, from the Atlantic to the Pacific.

The true, throbbing heart of Costa Rica does not beat above 5000 ft (1500 m) but spreads across the upland plain of the Meseta Central, the bastion where dreams have become reality. Here, around the second half of the 17th century, the Spanish colons succeeded in establishing themselves; having finally built up immunity against tropical disease, they penetrated into the tangled density of the jungle, where they founded the city of Cartago in 1563.

Contrary to what happened in Guatemala, Mexico and Panama, the native population in Cartago – as in the rest of Costa Rica – remained extremely small. This is why the *mestizo* culture, widely found elsewhere in Latin America, did not take root in this area. Even today, approximately 90% of the population is of Spanish descent, and therefore white and Catholic, 3% of African ancestry, 1% *Indios*, and the rest Chinese or other races. Cartago was totally destroyed during the 1723 eruption of Irazu volcano; rebuilt by the survivors, it remained the capital of Costa Rica until 1823 when the country, having obtained its independence from Spain in 1821, became a member state of the United Provinces of Central America. Over the years, violent earthquakes have wiped away much of its history, affecting almost all of its ancient and sacred buildings. Even the most famous church of Costa Rica, the Basilica de Nuestra Señora de Los Angeles, named for the country's patron saint, was destroyed in 1926 by volcanic fury and was then rebuilt in a Byzantine style.

In the course of the 18th century the colony began to expand, creating settlements in the fertile areas of the highland plains where, lulled by its perpetual spring climate,

20 top The basilica at Cartago is an important popular religious center.

20 bottom The interior of the Basilica de Nuestra Señora de Los Angeles, at Cartago, is extremely sumptuous and well preserved.

20 top The basilica at Cartago is an important popular religious center.

20 bottom The interior of the Basilica de Nuestra Señora de Los Angeles, at Cartago, is extremely sumptuous and well preserved.

21 The Basilica of Nuestra Señora de Los Angeles, in the city of Cartago, is the most famous in the country. Founded in 1635, it was totally destroyed by the earthquake of 1926 and has been subsequently rebuilt in Byzantine style.

approximately 60 percent of the population lives today. Heredia, an important cultural center for the country with its National University, Alajuela, like a perfumed tropical garden filled with butterflies and San José, the capital and nerve center of the nation, look out over the endless and prosperous coffee plantations. Stores, shopping malls, fast food chains and the traffic all dress San José in what seems to be an overcoat stitched in North America. "Our temples and palaces are nature itself," say the Costa Ricans and, in fact, even though founded in 1737, very few traces remain in the capital of the colonial era and of its sumptuous churches and Baroque palaces, razed to the ground by the frequent earthquakes. The Barrio Amón, the central neighborhood, has buildings dating back to the end of the century, San Pedro is crowded with energetic youth whilst La Sabana, the largest park in the city, is relentlessly cut off from the flow of the remorseless traffic. The prestigious Teatro Nacional building, constructed in 1897 and modeled on the Opéra in Paris, fascinates with its marbles, frescoes, crystals and its precious woods and alabasters, representing the New World's finest example of the Neo-Classical style. The most prominent, among the paintings to be found there, is an enormous canvas depicting the harvesting and export of coffee: painted in Italy at the end of the 19th century, it has been reproduced on the five *colones* banknote, which is considered to be among the finest in the world.

Of all the Central American countries, Costa Rica preserves the fewest signs of pre-Columbian culture: the civilizations which spread through Mexico in the northern part of Central America, including the Aztec and Mayan, did not penetrate much farther south. Such traces as were left of these peoples have been preserved in the Museo de Jade, the cradle of the world's most important pre-Colombian jade collection, and in the Museo de Oro Precolombino where approximately two thousand objects are on show for the appreciative wandering visitor.

The Museo Nacional, which houses several archaeological collections covering both the artistic and historic past of Costa Rica, is located within the Bellavista Fortress, the old military headquarters converted into a cultural center by President José Figueres Ferrer, who was known as Don Pepe. An upholder in 1949 of the new Costa Rican constitution, which still applies today, he ordered the dissolution of the armed forces, assigning both the money saved and the military buildings thus released to social and health services, culture and education. Even today, after half a century, Costa Rica is considered to be the most stable and secure nation of Latin America, where the only artillery accepted is the constant and incessant rumbling of its volcanoes. These may seem trivial matters, but they represent medals for valor in a Spanish America accustomed to coup d'états and dictatorships, racial problems and poverty. Wars have been kept at bay by men and prizes, such as the Nobel Peace Prize awarded in 1987 to Oscar Arias Sánchez, head of state from 1986 to 1990.

Thanks to its political stability, its presidents and the fierce yet sociable character of its inhabitants, Costa Rica has been awarded the diploma as American champion for sustainable development and responsible tourism, as well as the leadership in the coffee and banana trades. It was the construction of the railroad running from San José to the

Atlantic which gave rise, at the end of the 19th century, to the cultivation and trade in coffee and bananas. The Banana Republic was thus born: along with coffee, this fruit became the most important export, binding the country into a tight agreement with industrial and financial groups in the United States. The United Fruit Company, founded in 1899, built up huge wealth from the banana trade. This circumstance may well have inspired the imagination of Gabriel García Márquez when providing, in his novel *One Hundred Years of Solitude*, an accurate description of the machinations of American banana operators in an imaginary Latin-American city.

The gently descending coastal flanks hold in the mountainous outbreaks running from north to south through the entire country. East and west, two contrasting worlds, are near yet far; emotional and carefree. The Caribbean coast smiles, sings and dances along its beautiful beaches, its stretches of mangroves, its swampy forests and navigable canals. Approximately one half of the coastline is protected by two national parks and two wildlife reserves. And other languages can also be heard. One third of its inhabitants are in fact of Jamaican origin – descendants of workers on plantations and railways – while, farther south live several thousand Bribri and Cabecar *Indios*. To explore this area properly, the visitor does not need feet for walking but boats for navigating. The seaside waterways known as *los canales* push the mainland farther down the coast, thus providing an extended framework for unique opportunities. In addition to the Bara del Colorado wildlife reserve, on the border with Nicaragua, the Tortugero reduces even the most demanding spirit to silence.

22 *A pair of macaws, in the Osa Peninsula, with their typical scarlet-red plumage, contrasting strongly with the wide stripe of yellow across the central section of their wings. A characteristic of the red and yellow macaw, which has aroused the interest of ethologists, is the use of both claws for handling its food. The claw normally used by a bird for this purpose is just the left, while holding itself upright with the right.*

22-23 *The beaches to the south of the Caribbean coastline are bordered by palm trees and tropical forests which come right down to the shoreline. The* *whole area is notable for an unbroken string of coves, for its coral reefs lying close to the shore, and for its uncontaminated beaches.*

This national park has the unique honor of witnessing the magic of a night sky transformed into a planetarium: only a few privileged stars are allowed to fall and cling to the palms, decorating them with a timeless brilliance. High waves, strong currents and frequent roving sharks naturally convert the wide beaches of this park into a kingdom for turtles rather than bathers. During moonlit nights, at high tide, hundreds of turtles swim toward the beach, trudge onto the sand and dig with the utmost care tiny nests designed for their eggs. It is the universal maternal instinct, wrapped in the silent emotions of those who breathlessly watch. It is the great event of birth when, at the moment of hatching, the baby turtles make their way across the sand, drawn to the sea as if to a mirage. Many of these creatures, captured by birds or attacked by fish, never reach their desired destination. While these "green" turtles – observed and studied here since 1955 – prepare their nests in large groups and even in a single night emerge from the sea in their thousands, the "lute" turtle appears in solitude, burdened by a shell that can measure up to 5 ft (1.5 m) in length and weigh 800 lbs (360 kg).

Here in the Tortugero the animal population never finds itself alone. The light filtered by the rain forest's dense foliage presides over the slow-flowing dark waters of the canals. This is a magic and boundless Noah's Ark that opens its doors with a triumphant air. Strange spiders and capuchin monkeys leap from one branch to another, escorting the boats as they glide along the canals; large howlers bellow out their cries, perforating the forest air for up to half a mile (1 km); sloths, anteaters, razor-backs and tapirs coexist in the wild with jaguars, ocelots and pumas in this undisturbed territory in the dense Tortugero forest. Along the banks, the freshwater turtles lie warming themselves in the sun on tree trunks; when disturbed, they dive into the waters of the canals, becoming easy prey to the agile caymans and crocodiles.

Approximately 200 species of reptiles, half of them snakes, blend themselves into the green of the forest abandoning the scene to "Jesus," the lizard that runs across the surface of the water, and to the iguanas, miniature dinosaurs in search of a future. Leaping all around is a huge range of frogs and toads, including the poisonous dendrobatidae or dart frogs, much sought-after by the native population for poisoning the tips of their blowpipe darts. In addition to the two and four-footed varieties, the forest festivities draw in feathers and wings, hard beaks and colors, chirpings and trillings: whilst toucans, parrots and hummingbirds fly from one bank to another, cormorants and herons seek out prey, and kingfishers and frigate birds peer around in their search for love.

A similar, fantastic world is to be found along the coasts of the country where they dip into the Pacific Ocean. Approximately 210 sq. miles (543 sq. km) of uncontaminated rain forest, the finest on the entire west coast of Central America, are to be found on the Osa peninsula. Here in the Parque Nacional Corcovado, amid

*24-25 About 22 miles (36 km) from Samara, along the Pacific coast, the Ostional National Wildlife Refuge offers shelter to thousands of Olive Ridley sea turtles (*Lepidochelys olivacea*) as they emerge from the ocean to lay their eggs. This nocturnal spectacle can last for as long as three days.*

the thick vegetation, the ever-scary jaguar, which can weigh over 220 lbs (100 kg) and measure over 6 ft (2 m), peers out from among the leaves at a nearby prey that remains unaware of its silent presence. The monkeys do not hide, nor do they show signs of shyness: curiosity and speed keep them always alert and aware. In any roll call of this park an additional species steps up: the saimiri of Central America, also known as the squirrel monkey. Weighing in at less than 0.5 lbs (1 kg) and only about a 12 inches (30 cm) long, it is amongst the smallest monkey species on earth. And it's a real pest. It runs, jumps and hunts along the crests of the highest trees with unmatched agility and a whirling gait. In this park, one can have a close-up view of things otherwise virtually impossibile to see: three species of anteaters, sloths unmoving on branches or even upside down as they mimic the slow movements around them, the huge Baird's tapir with all of its 330-660 lbs (150-300 kg), or six different species of raccoons, also known as "wash bears" because of their unusual black masks which have earned them the title of "bandits of the forest."

The arches sketched out by the trees at a height of 130 ft (40 m) come to life with the flights of the largest colony of scarlet macaws to be found in Costa Rica and with the merry-go-round of the hummingbirds that, by beating their wings up to 80 times per second, remain motionless, even though they're flying.

But is seems truly regal music when the very rare, almost extinct harpy eagle makes its appearance, a bird of prey 3 ft tall (1 m) that whirls between the tops of the trees exhibiting unbelievable acrobatic skills. This is a whirlwind dance usually rewarded with a rich prize where, at times, sloths and monkeys have to admit a humiliating defeat.

The beach-side rain forests, banana and oil palm plantations line the Golfo Dulce down as far as Panama, but going north the visitor starts to see a dancing sequence of beaches, stretches of sand, tourists and surfers. There is no need to have seen the many surf movies to appreciate that it is precisely here, along the west coast of Costa Rica, that surfer fanatics have found their *puerto escondido*. From Canada, Europe, Hawaii and United States, they all meet here to await the perfect wave that rolls onto the beaches between Tamarindo and Cabo Blanco, to listen to the offshore winds, to ride the crests before the waves crash onto the shores of the Guanacaste Province, onto the bays of Conchal, Brasilito and Flamingo, and onto the Playa Carmen. The natives, more drawn to convenience than adventure, favor the beaches surrounding the main city of the central coast of the Pacific, Puntarenas, directly facing Playa Naranjo, and those of the Nicoya Peninsula. Here, in the 1950s, the Swede Olaf Wessberg bought a house and became a pioneering figure in the environmental culture of Costa Rica.

Wesberg was the man who managed to collect funds and contributions to set up the magnificent Cabo Blanco Natural Reserve, establishing severe and rigid protective measures that were only to be relaxed in the 1970s and 80s. It was then that the bulldozers brought destruction to the forests in the search for land to devote to livestock breeding. But for every error, for those that look, there is always a remedy. And Costa Rica has provided that remedy, earning the enthusiastic support of ecologists and winning an avalanche of compliments in the official reports of international bodies.

This coastline is swallowed up by the Pacific, but is also crossed by important waterways such as the Taracoles River, where hundreds of crocodiles, reaching up to 20 ft (6 m) in length, live alongside the horses and the oxen of nearby ranches. The white or black sandy beaches that extend from Playa Herradura to Dominical, are bordered by oil-palm plantations and flown over by flocks of brown pelicans, cormorants, gulls and frigate birds. This sandy expanse is broken up by the village of Quepos, an important center for sport fishing as well as providing the only access to a hilly area once unspoiled but today perfectly equipped to satisfy even the most demanding of tourists. And here we find ourselves a new monument to nature: the Manuel Antonio National Park, which has existed since 1972. This protected area may be the smallest in the country but is perhaps the most visited. The truly magnificent tropical beaches nestling up against the forests, the impressive rocky promontories that precipitate into the sea with such fierceness, the

abundance of animal wildlife and the three most beautiful inlets in the entire country, make it a center of wild activity in a basin of peace. Here, the animals astonish for their intimate relationship with man, so much better than many failed attempts at coexistence among humans: while monkeys rummage diligently in the trashcans and leaf-eating ants carefully redirect their routes to avoid an unwanted foot, iguanas beg for food as if they were small dogs and armadillos. Perhaps it is the only set of circumstances not strictly "ecological" in this country, otherwise completely in the hands of its trees, animals and volcanoes. Just like in a coup d'état. Except that we are not dealing here with men prevailing over other men. Instead, fire, air, water and land are the absolute proprietors of a wise and eternal place. These four elements mix smoothly together as in a painting, flowing along with the lava, sliding over the earth and reaching the sea. And finally taking to the air. Deafened by the gratitude of a humble but potent nature.

26-27 The warm waters and the year-round wave formations have made Escondida Beach, at Puntarenas, one of the beaches most frequented by surfers from around the world.

Located between the peninsulas of Nicoya and the more southerly Osa, the central Pacific coast tourist area is one of the most flourishing of Costa Rica.

28 This squirrel monkey is depicted on a tree of the forest in the Osa Peninsula. They normally live in groups of about 30 to 40, although they can sometimes reach 100.

28-29 The wild forests of the Manuel Antonio National Park also contain white beaches of quite outstanding beauty. There are archaeologists who maintain that

the half-circles of rock which emerge from the sea at low tide were in fact placed there by the Indios in pre-Columbian times to help trap the turtles.

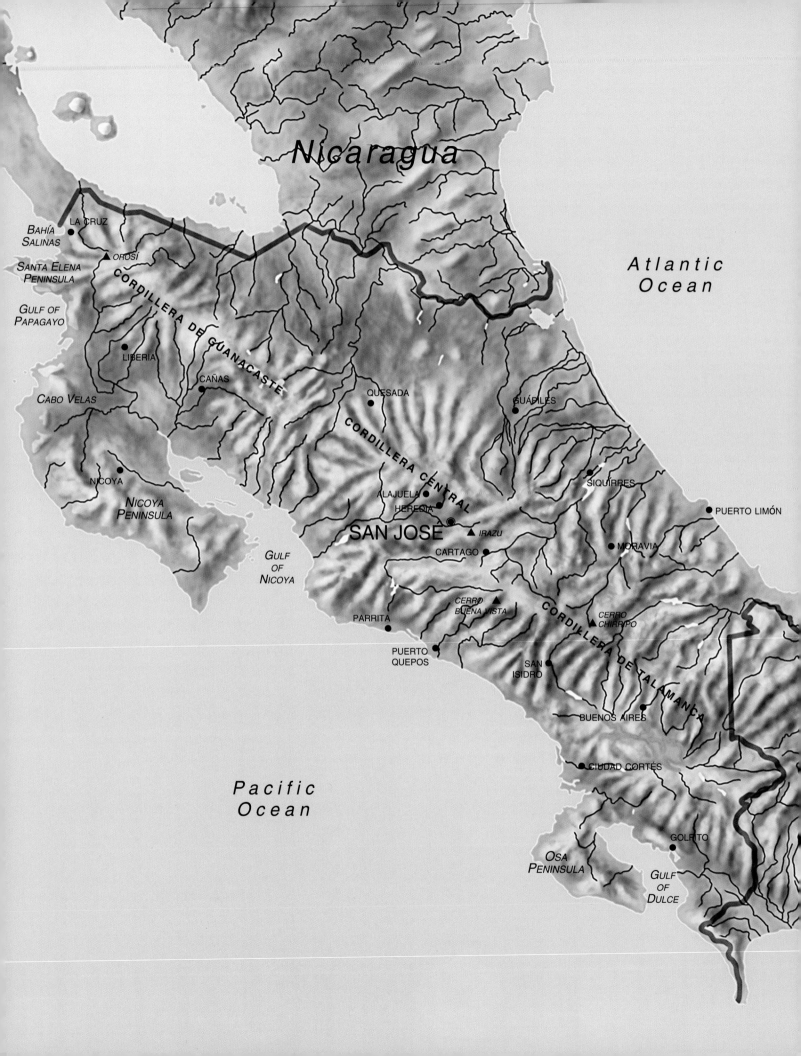

31 A waterfall cascades down into a small lake near the Rara Avis Research Station, within the tropical reserve of that same name. With its 2471 acres (1000 hectares), this undisturbed area is protected by a privately run enterprise aimed at protecting the more than 330 species of birds, apes, tapirs, felines, bromeliads and many others.

32-33 The Monteverde Cloud Forest Reserve, which is almost permanently shrouded in clouds, is the most famous of the humid rain forests located in the country. The dense vegetation, which can reach a height of 130 ft (40 m) offers a home to more than half of the animal and plant species of the country. This protected oasis was founded in the early 1950s by a group of a dozen or so North American Quaker families; this reserve continues to expand thanks to funding that continues to arrive from around the world.

*34-35 Known commonly by the locals as bocaracá (*Bothriechis schlegelii*), this eyelash viper is the smallest yet most poisonous of all Costa Rican snakes. It is mostly a nocturnal reptile and its poison, fatal to smaller prey, can cause severe problems to humans.*

Cities between Valleys and Mountains

36 top Immense sizes and fantastic shapes characterize the gardens decorating the square in front of a church in Zacero. This small town is located at the extreme western end of the Cordillera Central at a height of 5577 ft (1700 m) above sea level.

36 bottom A church of San José de la Montaña, a small village in the province of Heredia. This is an important cultural center in Costa Rica, with its National University, retaining more the typical atmosphere of a pueblo rather than that of a modern center.

37 The capital of San José is situated at a height of 3773 ft (1150 m) in the wide and fertile Central Valley, at the foot of the Cordillera Central. This location guarantees the city a pleasant and stable climate described by the inhabitants of San José, the "Joséfinos," as "eternal spring." The original urban nucleus of San José was laid down in the 18th century by the Spanish colonists. Alongside this grid-like urban layout with its architecture typical of any Spanish city, the visitor will notice much development and modern elements, such as the Banco Nacional skyscraper. One curious fact: there are no street names and numbers but merely references to road crossings and neighborhoods. Among the first things to study are the Spanish language and the cardinal points, useful for asking information from the very helpful Ticos population.

San José, Colonial Style and Modern Charm

38-39 The colonial style Central Post Office also houses the postal, telegraphic and philatelic museum. In Costa Rica the postal service is particularly efficient.

39 top San José's oldest public space is the Parque Central, always crowded because of the bus terminus and taxi area which service the needs of the entire city. Overlooking this square are the Metropolitan Cathedral and the Neo-Classical Melico Salazar Theater.

39 bottom Detail of the Central Bank of San José in the Banco Nacional building, the headquarters of the nation's most important bank. This building runs along the main street that crosses the city, the Paseo Colón.

40 The prestigious Teatro Nacional is considered to be the city's most impressive public building. Built in the final decade of the 19th century, it suffered severe damage in the 1991 earthquake but was subsequently meticulously restored.

41 top Overlooking the Parque Central, the Metropolitan Cathedral is the largest church of the city. Built in stone in 1871, it has been remodeled many times throughout the years and was fully restored in 1983, in time for the visit by Pope John Paul II.

41 bottom Of the paintings displayed in the vestibule of the Teatro Nacional, the most important depicts the harvesting and export of coffee. In 1968, this scene was reproduced on the 5 colones national banknote.

42 top The Museo de Los Niños is a museum strictly dedicated to science, art and geography and was designed specifically to provide a cultural appeal to the young. The museum makes use of a building that was once a prison.

42 center and bottom Within the large Parque La Sabana – the site of the capital's airport until 1955 – stands the Museo de Arte Costarricense, which houses a permanent collection of paintings and sculptures from the 19th and 20th centuries.

42-43 *The Edificio Metálico (Metal Building) owes its name to the immense quantity of metal used in its construction. Dating back to 1897, it is one of the oldest schools in the country and today houses the Escuela Buenaventura Corrales.*

Centers of Religion and Nature

44 The church of the Inmaculada Concepcíon at Heredia was built in 1797 and is still in use today.

44-45 It can be readily deducted from the number of churches throughout the country that Catholicism is the religion of the Ticos, the inhabitants of Costa Rica. Even small communities such as Zarcero, at the western extremity of the Cordillera Central, revolve around the church in the center of the village. This church, built in 1895 and dedicated to the Archangel St Rafael, contains numerous paintings among which stands out the series representing the Way of the Cross.

46 Sarchí, the most famous center in the country for artisan products, has also one of its most attractive churches. The city is divided by the River Trojas and extends for several miles along the main road linking Grecia to Naranjo, to the north west of San José.

46-47 The modest agricultural center of Grecia, in the province of Alajuela, is noted for its Metal Church, referred to by the inhabitants as the "red church" and used as a reference point for meetings and assemblies. Chosen in the past as the cleanest of all the small cities of Central America, the district of Grecia was founded in 1838 and today serves as an excellent base for tourist excursions to the Bosque Alegre natural shelter, just 5 miles (8 km) from the Poás volcano.

48-49 *A place of pilgrimage, the Basilica de Nuestra Señora de Los Angeles, at Cartago, is the best known church in the country. Every year large numbers of pilgrims leave San José on the 2nd of August to travel the 14*

miles (22 km) on foot in order to pray to the Virgin in the basilica. Cartago, located between the Cordillera Central and the mountain range of Talamanca, is the oldest city in the country.

49 top Inside the Basilica de Nuestra Señora de Los Angeles, at Cartago, is the famous Negrita, a statue associated with the Virgin who is the patron saint of the country. The Negrita is credited with miraculous curative powers, as evidenced by the numerous votive offerings left in gratitude.

49 bottom *The city of Heredia was founded by the Spanish in 1706, as can be seen from the colonial style of the buildings dating from that era which have survived the subsequent earthquakes. The tower dating from the colonial era, known as "El Fortín," is classified as a site of national historic interest.*

From Volcanoes to Forests

50 top The Poás Volcano National Park extends around the volcano of the same name. Over 8,800 ft (2704 m) high, the mountain has a crater almost a mile wide (1.5 km) and 950 ft (300 m) deep, and with its numerous active fumaroles and geysers is among the world's largest volcanoes. A record has been kept since 1828 of all its eruptions, the most recent occurring in 1989. From the summit there is a very attractive view over a small, mist-clad forest, home to many species of birds surviving among the bromeliads, mosses and lichens.

50 bottom The clouds are an essential feature of the humid tropical forest known as the Monteverde Cloud Forest Reserve. The lifting of these clouds provokes fascinating effects of light that appear to penetrate even the darkest corners of the dense undergrowth. Among these are the small natural pools at the feet of the waterfalls.

51 The red-eyed tree frogs (Agalychnis callidryas), *live near the waterways in the dense forest. They are multicolored amphibians: the predominant body color is a brilliant green, with huge red eyes and orange feet. The male is no different from the female in its coloring but is substantially smaller.*

52-53, 53 top right and 53 bottom right *The Braulio Carrillo National Park is crossed by the main state highway linking San José with the Caribbean coast. The untamed land bordering the road takes in a range of altitudes: from the 164 ft (50 m) of the Caribbean plains rising to 9514 ft (2900 m) at the summit of the Barva volcano. Because of this variety of altitudes and climates, the Braulio Carrillo accommodates a notable variety of habitats and of species of flora and fauna. Among the animal populations can be found felines, tapirs, razor-backs, sloths, monkeys and an incredible number of birds of every species. The rich vegetation is covered with epiphytes, while the flora buried in the undergrowth of the forest applies itself to maximizing the process of photosynthesis even in conditions of poor light.*

53 left *The most obvious identifying feature of the Costa Rican toucan is its very pronounced, but at the same time very light, colored beak. This protuberance is in fact* *almost totally hollow, supported internally by a spongy mesh of bony material. The toucans live in the treetops, nesting in tree-trunk hollows.*

53 center right *The terrain of this rain forest is relatively low in nutritional content. The extensive root systems of many plants are directed toward providing the maximum of support but with the minimum of penetration in the soil. This phenomenon is made possible by extracting nutriment through the recycling of decomposed material drawn from the upper reaches of the trees.*

54-55 *The vertebrate predators most commonly found in the habitat of the forest are the snakes, which are able to camouflage themselves by merging into their background. In Costa Rica 220 species of reptiles have been counted in a census, of which 8 appear to be facing extinction.*

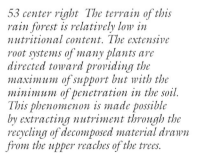

56 top left Squirrels are commonly found throughout the continent, but the red-tailed squirrel (Sciurus granatensis) lives mostly in tropical zones.

56 top right There are vividly colored birds identifiable by their long tails; the motmot (Momotus momota) of this country is found in 6 separate species.

56 bottom Bird watching is much practiced in all of Costa Rica's protected areas. More than 800 identified species of birds have been classified through the various altitudes and habitats of the country.

56-57 The brown-throated three-toed sloth (Bradypus variegatus) is a day-time mammal, commonly seen in the Corcovado National Park on the Osa peninsula. The females hold their young clutched to their breast for periods often in excess of five months.

58 top left and right The Tapantí National Park is located on the northern slopes of the Cordillera de Talamanca, in a wild and humid area covered by rain forest. The heavy rain in the area creates numerous watercourses and waterfalls which render the terrain almost impenetrable. The footpaths may be few but they remain a strong attraction for bird-watching enthusiasts. More than 200 species of bird are to be found in this area, including the famous quetzal, a legendary bird found throughout Central America as far north as Mexico.

60-61 After every downpour, the Costa Rican sky immediately gives way to bright sunlight creating the magical phenomenon of the rainbow. Given the frequency of these deluges – the average annual rainfall is in excess of 100 in. (2,500 mm) – the rainbows are considered a permanent feature of this scenery.

58 bottom Mushrooms are a crucial element in the life cycle of the rain forest. They fulfill the important functions of decomposing the trees, branches and leaves as the fall to the ground, initiating a regeneration process essential for the survival of the forest itself.

59 Known as Jesus because of its ability to "walk" on water, the common basilisk (Basiliscus basiliscus) belongs to the iguana family. It can grow to a length of 31 in. (80 cm), but this includes the tail amounting to two-thirds of the total body. The younger specimens, being lighter, can run for up to 110 yards (100 m) on the surface of the water. This "miracle" results from its ability to rise to a semi-erect position on its webbed back feet, using its long tail as a balancing mechanism. The males are recognizable by a very pronounced crest which makes them look like small dinosaurs.

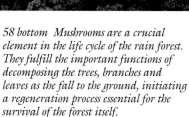

62 The waterfalls generated by the rivers of the vast territories that run down from the heights of the Cordillera Central to the Atlantic plains bordering Nicaragua are numerous and spectacular. The highway that leaves San José, passing between the Poás and Barva volcanoes, reaches the height of over 6500 ft (2000 m) before descending through uncontaminated tropical rain forests of intense humidity all the way to the valleys of the La Paz and Sarapiquí rivers. This route takes in a number of waterfalls, including the impressive Catarata La Paz in the vicinity of Vara Blanca.

63 Within the privately owned Rara Avis reserve, located on the eastern slopes of the Cordillera Central, is an 180 ft (55 m) waterfall that slashes the rain forest in two. At its foot, a number of pools have formed where one can bathe surrounded by an uncontaminated natural environment.

64-65 The intense rainfalls of Costa Rica give rise to numerous water courses which are vital for the maintenance of the rainforest. Along the banks of the Rio Sarapiquí is the Selva, a privately owned estate covering some 3500 acres (1600 hectares) of humid tropical forest where a center for biological research is based.

Volcanoes: the Kingdom of Craters and Red-Hot Lava

66-67 and 68-69 The Arenal volcano is one of the world's most active. Its volcanic activity is always constant, as demonstrated by the immense clouds of ash hurled into the air by powerful explosions.

67 top The imposing Poás volcano, situated in the national park of the same name, is 8870 ft (2704 m) high. The crater is a permanently bubbling, smoke-filled cauldron 1000 ft (300 m) deep; the water that accumulates at its bottom regularly explodes in columns of steam.

67 bottom The country around the crater of the Irazu volcano, which rises to 11,440 ft (3432 m), has a moon-like quality.

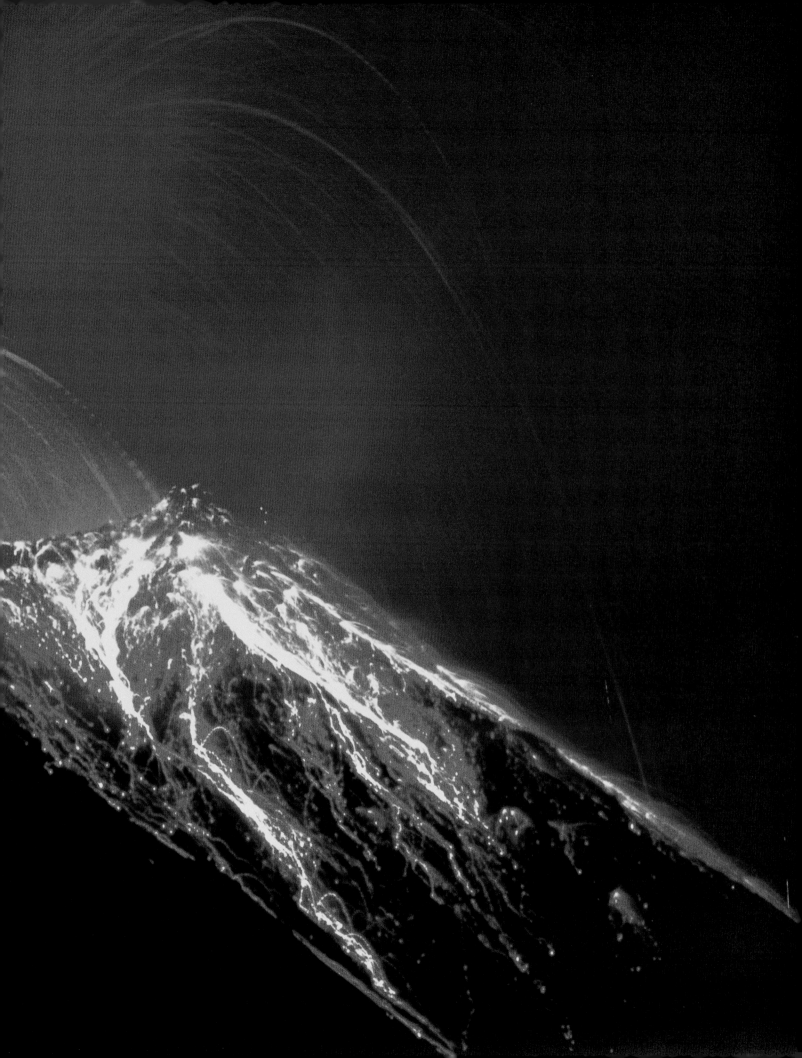

Wild Life in Technicolor

70 top right Among all the fascinating butterflies, the morpho (Morpho peleides) offers a particularly blinding impact because of the electric blue of its wings. Its 7 in. (15 cm) wingspan makes it readily visible along the rivers and in the forests of the country.

70 bottom Adaptive mimetism is of critical importance for the survival of many insects. Choosing the leaves on which to settle is a refined art that the butterflies know well. To deceive the predators is a must, so much so that some moths can even take on the appearance of poisonous creatures.

70 top left and 71 Over 3000 species of butterfly have been identified in Costa Rica, about 10% of the total butterfly types existing in the world. They can, in fact, be seen fluttering around throughout the country, from mountain summits to the coastal plains of both oceanic coastlines. The "mariposari," as the tropical gardens dedicated to the butterfly are known, are frequently encountered in Costa Rica: hundreds of butterflies of every species can be observed in all phases of their complex life cycles.

72-73 The country can number among its most famous birds some 50 species of hummingbirds. This specimen of stripe-tailed hummingbird (Eupherusa eximia), differing from the others by the coloring of its tail, feeds on the nectar of a lily-like flower.

73 top The green violet-ear hummingbird (Colibrí thalassinus) is a species that lives at high altitudes and that is only found in the humid, tropical forests. Because of their ability to beat their wing up to 80 times per second, hummingbirds are famous for being the only species in the world able to hang motionless in flight and even to fly backwards.

73 bottom This magenta-throated woodstar hummingbird (Calliphlox bryantae) is intent on feeding from the nectar of the poinsettia (Euphorbia pulcherrima). Its typically long and slender beak allows this bird to explore the profoundest depths of the flower in its search for nectar.

74 top The most highly developed sense of the red-eyed tree frog (Agalychnis callidryas) is undoubtedly its sight: this animal in fact has a parabolic view of everything that surrounds it. It also has a well-developed sense of touch which, thanks to its sucker pads, enables it to climb even the smoothest surfaces of the vegetation.

74 bottom The humid forest of Monteverde used to be the only place in the world to see the tiny golden toad (Bufo periglenes). This amphibious species became extinct in 1989, because of its extreme sensitivity to the global pollution in the air. These frogs, breathe using both their primitive lungs and also through their skin, which renders them extremely vulnerable.

75 The tree frogs of the rain forests have huge eyes and long legs which end in sucker pads. They feed on insects and live predominantly in the trees without fear of falling. These pads allow them to adhere to even the smoothest foliage.

76-77 Snakes constitute at least one half of the more than 200 reptile species found in the country. Though much talked about they are very rarely seen; they are mainly nocturnal and non-aggressive, therefore if disturbed they prefer to slither away to avoid being approached. They hide under flowers and leaves and this is a good reason for being particularly careful if not accompanied by a guide.

*77 top The preferred habitat of the
bocaracá, or eyelash viper (Bothriechis
schleglii), is the dense leafy growths of the
palm trees, which has therefore earned it
its popular title of "palm tree viper."
With its triangular-shaped head and
modest length, rarely reaching 30 in.
(75 cm), the bocaracá is the smallest of
the country's snakes: they give birth each
year to about a dozen young.*

77 bottom Known as the ojo de gato
(Imantodes cenchoa), *this snake lives
in the lower and middle reaches of the
forest preferring epiphyte plants,
including the bromeliad flowers, for its
support. Small and slender, this serpent
has a particularly thin neck and a
head provided with protruding eyes.*

78 There are 3 species of anteaters
to be found in the country, the
commonest of which is the tamandua
(Tamandua mexicana) known for
its black and gold cape-like back.
It stands about 5 ft tall (1.5 m) and
weighs between 9 and 18 lbs (4 to
8 kg). Its tongue, which can be up to
16 in. long (40 cm), is covered with
microscopic spikes which help to direct
the food toward its mouth.

78-79 Included in the feline
population of the Costa Rican forests
is the ocelot (Felis pardalis), an
animal similar to the jaguar. It is
much the same color but is smaller
with a tail shorter than its hind legs.
Though more numerous than the
jaguar, it is nevertheless very shy
and rarely lets itself be seen.

*80-81 This tiny and curious white-headed capuchin (*Cebus capucinus*) is one of the most easily seen monkeys in the forests of Costa Rica. They hunt in packs through the thick vegetation in their search for fruit and insects, showing off their somewhat curious predatory instincts. Possessors of a long prehensile tail, they often wrap this around themselves to produce a curious curl-like effect.*

*81 The howler monkey (*Alouatta palliata*), which weighs around 18 lbs (8 kg), is the larges of the apes found in Costa Rica. It is usually heard long before it can actually be seen. The loud roars of this ape species can be heard over half a mile away (1 km), even in the densest of forests. They tend to stay within their own territory, living in groups of about 12 in the forest treetops.*

An Endless Rainbow

82 The road which heads south from Puerto Limón runs parallel to the wild coastline of the southern Caribbean plains as far as the border with Panama. There are several differences between the much-indented and fragmented coastline of the west and its eastern equivalent, with its more gentle beaches adorned with coral reef; the climate, humid and rainy throughout the year, sustains the swampy forests along the shoreline.

83 The much-indented shoreline of the Pacific coast lines the great bay of the Nicoya Peninsula in the Gulf of Papagayo. We are in the province of Guanacaste, where the most sheltered of the beaches is Playa Panamá; with its long stretch of dark sand, it has been transformed in recent times into a tourist center to the detriment of the dry, tropical forest. This site is next to the much more renowned northern beaches, such as Playa Hermosa, Playa del Coco and Ocotal.

Pacific Coast, a Triumph of the Wilderness

84 top The beach at Guacamaya, in the province of Guanacaste, looks out onto the Pacific Ocean, and is surrounded by extremely dense vegetation which comes right down to the thin strips of white beach close to the water's edge. Contrasts between the colors are particularly marked here, although always a common experience in Costa Rica.

84 center The Santa Rosa National Park, the first as well as the largest protected area in Costa Rica, occupies the greater part of the Santa Elena Peninsula, located in the extreme northwest of the country. Here is the Playa Sancite, chosen by many species of sea turtles for depositing their eggs. During the rainy season,

especially in the months of September and October, Playa Nancite is transformed into the most sought-after meeting place for thousands of olive ridley turtles coming here from all over the tropical zone of the Pacific. This area too is covered by Central America's largest expanse of dry, tropical forest.

84 bottom and 84-85 Looking out onto the Pacific, all along the Nicoya Peninsula in the province of Guanacaste, are the most important seaside resorts. The major attractions of this naturalistic and tourist area are the wild and deserted beaches, backed by the forest.

86 top The coasts of the Osa Peninsula are part of the protected Corcovado National Park and contain quite the best coastal rain forests on the western side of Central America. The varied habitats to be found there guarantee the survival of a rich and diversified fauna.

86 bottom The Bahía Ballena is the largest bay along the southern coast of the Nicoya Peninsula and is an excellent spot for whale sightings. The long beaches along the inner sections of the bay are well protected from the currents of the Pacific Ocean and therefore provide excellent vantage points for the passing of these giants of the sea.

86-87 Witch's Rock, in the Santa Rosa National Park, is one of the most sought-after destinations for surfers from all over the world. It is located along Tamarind Beach, which was once a fishing village in the northern part of Guanacaste, but has now become one of the most highly developed tourist centers of northern Costa Rica.

88 top One of the most spectacular members of the parrot family to be found in Costa Rica is the macaw, unmistakable by the 32 in (80 cm) of ultra-vibrant red coloring of its body and tail, the blue and yellow of its wings and the white of its face. They fly in small groups or in couples and, once paired off, stay together for life.

89 The keel-billed toucan (Ramphastos sulfuratus) is a regular inhabitant of the northern coastal forests of Guanacaste. The somewhat larger Swainson's toucan (Ramphastos swainsonii), on the other hand, prefers the high trees found in the humid forests of the South Pacific.

88 bottom The Corcovado accommodates felines, crocodiles, peccaries, giant anteaters, jaguars and Baird's tapirs, as well as over 400 types of birds amongst which can be found numerous species of the brown pelican which normally station themselves on rocky outcrops of the seabed.

90-91 The Pacific coastline of Costa Rica is the only place in the world where the humpback whales (Megaptera novaeangliae) travel in from both hemispheres, north and south, to produce and nurture their young. This migratory custom also accounts for the longest-lasting whale-watching season in the world. Along the Drake Bay coast, in the Puntarenas province, are some of the best spots for sighting these whales as they follow a migratory course, in groups of up to 15, down these coastal waters.

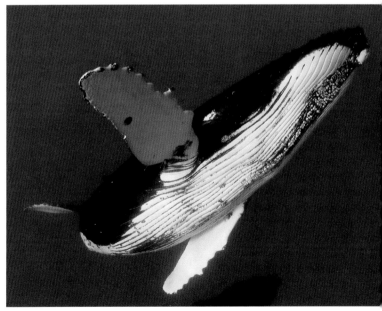

91 The most distinctive identifying feature of the humpback whale is the length of its pectoral fin, which can measure up to 17 ft (5 m). These mammals are capable of several acrobatic tricks: they can roll, beat their fins on the water and, alone among the Mysticeti species, leap completely out of the sea.

The Caribbean Coast: "Pura Vida"

92 The majority of the turtle species inhabiting the seas along the Caribbean coast meet annually on the uncontaminated beaches of the protected area of Tortuguero.

92-93 Slipping along the channels of Tortuguero, overlooked by the dense canopy of the rain forest, the visitor can easily glimpse of a variety of habitats with a breathtaking range of animal species. To stroke a fresh water turtle is to attract the immediate attention of the caymans who come scurrying to the boat while the spiteful spider monkeys swing from tree to tree, following the boat throughout its journey.

94-95 The Gandoca-Manzanillo National Wildlife Refuge follows the Caribbean coast as far as the Panamanian border. This vast territory takes in over 20 sq. miles (52 sq. km) of sea and provides protection to the coral reef just 650 ft (200 m) offshore. The luxuriant rain forest presses around uncontaminated beaches, bordered by coconut palms, to create a particularly impressive tropical spectacle. A mysterious and fascinating red mangrove swamp is also found in the reserve.

95 Playa Uva is one of the most attractive beaches in the area around Puerto Viejo de Talamanca, a small village located at the southern end of the Atlantic coast. This coastline is much frequented by surfers because of its regular wave patterns but also for the liveliness and cheerfulness that pervade the locality.

96 *A study of the coral barriers of Cahuita and Gandoca has identified more than 30 different species of coral, more than 100 varieties of mollusc, some 40 different shellfish and at least 100 different types of fish. The best time to explore this ocean floor is in the months of March and April, when the discharges from the rivers, which empty into the sea in this area, are at their lowest leading to an improvement in the visibility, which is much more limited during the rest of the year.*

96-97 *The largest coral reef in Costa Rica lies in Punta Cahuita, to the north of Puerto Viejo. Unfortunately the reef suffered considerable damage during the 1991 earthquake. The whole coastline was in fact raised by about 3 ft (1 m), leaving the entire reef without water. It still remains a worthwhile place to visit for snorkelling enthusiasts.*

Isla del Coco: the Mysterious Isle

98 top Isla Manuelita is a small rocky formation to the north of Isla del Coco, inhabited only by hundreds of bird species. Since there are no landing spots, the birds can live and nest undisturbed.

98 bottom and 98-99 Isla del Coco is a small and mysterious island situated in the mid-Pacific Ocean more than 300 miles (500 km) off the coast of Costa Rica. In 1997, because of its isolation and unspoiled state, UNESCO designated it as a Patrimony of Humanity. The island's history is irretrievably linked to piracy and the countless treasures reputedly hidden there are still being sought today.

100-101 Notwithstanding their threatening appearance, the giant tropical moray eels will react only if disturbed, attacking with painful and lacerating bites. Normally their mouths will be open, not because they are always on the brink of war but because they open and close their jaws to breathe.

101 The coral reefs that surround Isla del Coco are known worldwide for the richness of their marine life: sergeant fish, blue striped grunts, sea turtles and white fin sharks, while shoals of silver Carangidaes populate the stony depths, the open waters and the submerged pinnacles.

102-103 The whale shark (Rhincodon typus) is one of the longest-lived sharks on the planet: some specimens can live for more than 100 years. It is the largest fish known to man at the present time, with some specimens reaching as much as 60 ft (18 m) in length. Notwithstanding it size, this is a totally harmless marine animal and in fact feeds by gathering in plankton and small fish as it swims along open-mouthed, passing the water through a filtering mechanism located in its gills.

103 Devil fish, hammer sharks and sailfish are amongst the larger creatures populating the waters around Isla del Coco. Great speed, elegance, and bizarre shapes are the identifying features of these three marine animals.

Between Smiles and Folklore

104 top As a small grocery store, the pulperia *supplies all the needs of a small village. In even the most remote areas, whether along the coast or well into the hinterland, this shop will be the only place supplied with a telephone, and often serves as a meeting place for the villagers.*

104 bottom *Horses are very much part of the rural life typical of the country and are the key players of the rodeos held in conjunction with agricultural shows and other special events.*

105 *One third of the inhabitants of the Caribbean coast are of Jamaican extraction, descendants of the workers employed in railway construction or in the plantations. In October, during the Día de las Culturas, a whole week is taken up with celebrations of the historic landing of Christopher Columbus. The roads of Puerto Limón are enlivened by a carnival with its rich parades in traditional costumes, dancing and singing.*

"Pura vida," between smiles and folklore

106 top A rodeo in the Guanacaste region: during the show, cowboys demonstrate their abilities by riding their horses in front of a crowd of locals and visitors.

106 bottom During the annual agricultural fair in the city of San Isidro del General numerous rodeos and bullfights are held in which everyone can participate. This agricultural center, located about 80 miles (130 km) from San José, is surrounded by coffee plantations, ranches and nurseries.

106-107 On July 25, Liberia, a city with a strongly rural nature, holds its Guanacaste celebration, putting on an impressive horseback parade, livestock auctions and bullfights.

108 top left and bottom El Día del Boyero *is a holiday in honor of the oxcart drivers with colorful parades of wagons and folkloristic dancing.*

108 top right The Fiesta de los Diablitos *is an indigenous festivity celebrated in many localities of the* country *and is a reminder of the struggle of the Indios against the Spanish conquerers. The most important of such events is held in the Boruca Indigenous Reserve, where pipes and drums accompany the Indios' dances, with their large wooden masks.*

109 Throughout the last week of the year even San José, the capital of Costa Rica, gives itself over to festivities, organizing numerous events and dances in traditional costumes.

110 and 110-111 The Fiesta de la Virgen del Mar *is celebrated on the waters of the Puntarenas seaport, the capital of the region bearing that name, which extends from the Gulf of Nicoya to the Panamanian border. The procession in honor of the Virgin of the Sea takes place in July and involves a parade of rowboats and motorboats, all scrupulously decorated to catch the festival spirit. Many other old traditional-style boats take to the waters of the gulf, following the peninsula's coastline.*

112, 112-113 and 114-115 The symbol of Costa Rican craftsmanship are the carretas, *the old agricultural carts now transformed into artistic and decorative works of art. The main center of this tradition is the small city of Sarchí, famous for its traditional crafts. These wooden carts exist in a variety of sizes and local artisans decorate them with small meticulous designs and vivid colors. This particular artistic tendency is also found in the flourishing production of ceramics which reproduce images from the pre-Columbian era, a source of pride in this region of Guanacaste.*

116 top The pineapples that reach our tables very often come from Costa Rica's tropical plantations.

116 center During the 19th century, the great coffee plantations of the fertile plains of the central upland areas transformed Costa Rica into a prosperous nation. The nation's most significant period of the economic and cultural growth is associated with Juan Rafáel Mora, who became president in 1849.
A well-known coffee producer, he ruled the country for 10 years.

116 bottom and 116-117 What most typifies the Caribbean coast, from Puerto Limón down to the border with Panama, is the literal carpeting of bananas; their impact has earned the country the title of "Banana Republic."

118-119 and 119 top The waterfalls of Costa Rica can be enjoyed in a variety of ways: they can be viewed from a distance or can be experienced by bathing in their thermal basins, such as those of the Tabacón Hot Springs, at the foot of the Arenal volcano.

119 bottom Small boats are often the only means of penetrating Costa Rica's wilder areas. The dense network of navigable canals of the Tortuguero and the numerous waterways giving access from both coastlines, often creating mangrove swamps along the way, are the only means of penetrating these mysterious locations.

120-121 The many rivers that flow down to the coast from the central mountain ranges offer ideal opportunities for rafting. The best-known rivers that are practicable all year round, with various degrees of difficulty, are the Río Reventazón and the Río Pacuare, both located on the Caribbean side.

122-123 *The multicolored pyramids of fruit on the stalls brighten up the roads linking the capital to the coasts. These are excellent places to stop and enjoy fresh fruit* batidas; *satisfaction is also guaranteed by the* pipas, *green coconuts pierced with a machete so that the juice can be drunk through a straw, directly from the nut.*

123 *Selling points for car tires on the Carretera Interamericana, which crosses the country from Nicaragua to Panama, are an absolute must. As well as being pitted with holes because of the abundant year-round rainfall, roads throughout the country are narrow and poorly signposted. To cross the country without having to change at least one tire is practically impossible.*

124 top A crowded and lively market extends along a central avenue in San José. The numerous stalls display agricultural produce coming directly from the neighboring fincas.

124 bottom and 124-125 Fruit is never lacking in Costa Rica, and it is an excellent nutrient to combat the tropical climate of the hotter days. Even the most isolated villages of the countryside have a shop or stall offering refreshing fruit.

126 Liberia, the capital of the province of Guanacaste, was founded in the mid-18th century. The city had 4000 inhabitants in 1864; only a tenth of them lived within it, the rest resided in the immediately surrounding countryside in typically highly colored houses.

127 top The village of Montezuma, just 7 miles (11 km) from the Cabo Blanco Absolute Nature Reserve and not far from Puntarenas, is especially popular with visitors because of its atmosphere reminiscent of the 1970s, of the friendly and cheerful nature of its people and of the walks that can be taken in the surrounding dense and humid forests.

127 bottom Those looking for a meal near the Poás volcano will be directed to a restaurant completely smothered in tourists' visiting cards, a strong invitation to sample its quality and take in the cheerful atmosphere.

128 Emblematic of local craftsmanship, these carved and colorful carts were traditionally used by the local countrymen. The themes most often represented include flowers, personalities, costumes and animals.

Photo Credits:

page 1: Michael & Patricia Fogden/Getty Images
pages 2-3: Marco Corsetti
pages 4-5: Michael & Patricia Fogden/Getty Images
page 6: Sue Cunningham/DanitaDelimont.com
page 7: Schafer & Hill/Getty Images
pages 8-9: Danny Lehman/Corbis
pages 10-11: Gail Shumway/Getty Images
pages 12-13: Christian Heeb/Agefotostock/Marka
page 14: Vincenzo Paolillo
pages 14-15: Jim Wark
page 16: Kevin Schafer/Corbis
page 17 top: Jack Hoehn/Index Stock/Corbis
page 17 bottom: Michael & Patricia Fogden/Getty Images
page 18: Armando Del Vecchio
pages 18-19: Juan José Pucci
page 20 top: Gustavo Valle
page 20 bottom: Rodrigo Barsallo
page 21: Juan José Pucci
page 22: Roy Toft/National Geographic Image Collection
pages 22-23: Juan José Pucci
pages 24-25: Doug Perrine/SeaPics.com

pages 26-27: Andres Garcia
page 28: Roy Toft/National Geographic Image Collection
pages 28-29: Alvaro Leiva
pages 30 and 31 left: Angelo Colombo/Archivio White Star
page 31 right: Stephen Alvarez/National Geographic Image Collection
pages 32-33: Sergio Pucci
pages 34-35: Gregory Basco/Deep Green Photography
page 36 top: Held/Agefotostock/Marka
page 36 bottom: Gustavo Valle
page 37: José Fuste Raga/Corbis
pages 38-39: Sue Cunningham/DanitaDelimont.com
page 39 top: José Fuste Raga/Agefotostock/Marka
page 39 bottom: Frank Scott
page 40: Dave G. Houser/Corbis
page 41 top: Juan José Pucci
page 41 bottom: Hepworth Images
page 42 top: Juan José Pucci

page 42 center and bottom: Marco Saborio
pages 42-43: Juan José Pucci
page 44: Clive Sawyer/PCL
pages 44-45: José Fuste Raga/Agefotostock/Marka
page 46: Frans Lemmens/zefa/Corbis
pages 46-47: Patrick Frilet/Hemis.fr
pages 48-49: Hepworth Images
page 49 top: Hepworth Images
page 49 bottom: AISA
page 50 top: Reinhard Dirscherl/Seapics.com
page 50 bottom: Buddy Mays/Corbis
page 51: Peter Lilja/Agefotostock/Marka
pages 52-53: Juan Manuel Borrero/Naturepl.com/Contrasto
page 53 top: Michael & Patricia Fogden/Getty Images
page 53 center left: P. Lavoretti/Panda Photo
page 53 center right: Gary Baasch/Corbis
page 53 bottom: Gary Baasch/Corbis
pages 54-55: Michael & Patricia Fogden/Getty Images
page 56 top left and right: Michael & Patricia Fogden/Getty Images
page 56 bottom: Konrad Whote
pages 56-57: Kevin Schafer/Corbis
page 58 top left: Peter Christopher/Masterfile/Sie
page 58 top right: Lynn M. Stone/Naturepl.com/Contrasto
page 58 bottom: Roy Toft/Getty Images
page 59: Joe McDonald/Corbis
pages 60-61: Kevin Schafer
page 62 top: Konrad Whote
page 62 bottom: Gerry Ellis/Getty Images
page 63: Juan José Pucci
pages 64-65: Michael & Patricia Fogden/Getty Images
pages 66-67: Kevin Schafer/Corbis
page 67 top: Kevin Schafer/NHPA/Photoshot Photo
page 67 bottom: Catherine Jouan – Jeanne Ruis/Jacana/HachettePhotos/Contrasto
pages 68-69: Kevin Schafer
page 70 top left: Gregory Basco/Deep Green Photography
page 70 top right: Michael & Patricia Fogden/Getty Images
page 70 bottom: Kevin Schafer/Corbis
page 71: Michael & Patricia Fogden/Getty Images
pages 72-73: Michael & Patricia Fogden/Corbis
page 73 top: Michael & Patricia Fogden/Corbis
page 73 bottom: Michael & Patricia Fogden/Getty Images
page 74 top: Franco Piemontesi
page 74 bottom: Michael & Patricia Fogden/Corbis
page 75: Steve Winter/Getty Images
pages 76-77: Norbert Wu/Getty Images
page 77 top: Michael & Patricia Fogden/Corbis
page 77 bottom: Joe McDonald/Corbis
page 78: Michael & Patricia Fogden/Corbis
pages 78-79: Alan Carey/Corbis Sygma/Corbis
pages 80-81: Wolfgang Kaehler/Corbis
page 81: Alan Carey/Corbis Sygma/Corbis
page 82 top: Juan José Pucci
page 82 bottom: Purestock/Getty Images
page 83: Sergio Pucci
page 84 top: Sergio Pucci
page 84 center: Kevin Schafer
page 84 bottom: Marco Corsetti
pages 84-85: Sergio Pucci

page 86 top: Gary Braasch/Corbis
page 86 bottom: Juan José Pucci
pages 86-87: Marco Corsetti
page 88 top: Kevin Schafer
page 88 bottom: Gary Braasch/Corbis
page 89: Kevin Schafer
pages 90-91: Doug Perrine/SeaPics.com
page 91 top and bottom: Masa Ushioda/SeaPics.com
page 92 top: F. Bruemmer/Panda Photo
page 92 bottom: Martin Wendler/NHPA/Photoshot Photo
pages 92-93: Bob Kirst/Corbis
pages 94-95: Sergio Pucci
page 95 top: Juan José Pucci
page 95 bottom: Michel Troncy/Hoa-Qui/HachettePhotos/Contrasto
page 96 top: Marine Themes
page 96 center and bottom: Brandon Cole
pages 96-97: Sergio Pucci
page 98 top: Vincenzo Paolillo
page 98 bottom: Jeff Rotman
pages 98-99: Vincenzo Paolillo
pages 100-101: Jeff Rotman
page 101 top: Kurt Amsler
page 101 center left and right: Vincenzo Paolillo
page 101 bottom: Vincenzo Paolillo
pages 102-103 Marine Themes
page 103 top: Marine Themes
page 103 center: Amos Nochoum/Corbis
page 103 bottom: Jeff Rotman
page 104 top Sylvain Grandadam/Agefotostock/Contrasto
page 104 bottom: Atlantide Phototravel/Corbis
page 105: Ian Cumming/Axiom Photographic
page 106 top: Martin Rogers/Corbis
page 106 bottom: Tony Arruza/Corbis
page 106-107: Martin Rogers/Corbis
page 108 top left: Sergio Pucci
page 108 top right: Juan José Pucci
page 108 bottom: OmniPhoto/De Bellis
page 109: Sergio Pucci
page 110 top, center and bottom: Sylvia Guardia
pages 110-111: Sylvia Guardia
page 112 top: Jan Butchofsky-Houser/Corbis
page 112 bottom: Patrick J. Endres/AlaskaPhotoGraphics.com
pages 112-113: Kevin Schafer/Corbis
pages 114-115: Juan José Pucci
page 116 top: John Coletti/JAI/Corbis
page 116 center and bottom: Martin Rogers/Corbis
pages 116-117: John Coletti/JAI/Corbis
pages 118-119: Michel DeYoung/Corbis
page 119 top: Atlantide Phototravel/Corbis
page 119 bottom: R H Productions/Robert Harding World Imagery/Corbis
pages 120-121: Kevin Schafer
pages 122-123 Danny Lehman/Corbis
page 123: Ian Cumming/Axiom Photographic
page 124 top: Ian Cumming/Axiom Photographic
page 124 bottom: Alvaro Leiva/Agefototock/Marka
pages 124-125: Asdrúbal LEIVA COTO
page 126: Ian Cumming/Axiom Photographic
page 127 top: Hauser/laif/Contrasto
page 127 bottom: Sylvain Grandadam/Agefotostock/Contrasto
page 128: Jan Butchofsky/Corbis

The author wishes to thank Vanessa Volonté for her collaboration